the guardian angel

oracle guidebook

connect with your guardian angels
for wisdom and guidance

delia ciccarelli

CICO BOOKS
LONDON NEW YORK

Published in 2022
by CICO Books
An imprint of Ryland Peters
& Small Ltd

20–21 Jockey's Fields
London WC1R 4BW

341 E 116th St
New York, NY 10029

www.rylandpeters.com

10 9 8 7 6 5 4 3 2 1

Text and illustrations
© Delia Ciccarelli 2022
Design © CICO Books 2022

ISBN: 978-1-80065-085-5

Printed in China

Commissioning editor:
Kristine Pidkameny
Senior commissioning editor:
Carmel Edmonds
Senior designer: Emily Breen
Art director: Sally Powell
Head of production:
Patricia Harrington
Publishing manager: Penny Craig
Publisher: Cindy Richards

Contents

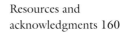

Introduction

The guardian angel oracle cards are a mystical and fascinating divinatory deck. Angels are otherworldly creatures of light, acting as intermediaries between the world of human beings and the divine.

Each of us has a guardian angel, who accompanies us throughout our life. Whether we are believers in God or not, the guardian angels exist—they are there every day to assist us and shine light in our life. Once contact has been made with them, the angels bring joy and serenity to those who have called them. These divine creatures manifest themselves to us only if invoked (see page 9). Do not hesitate to appeal to the angels—your guardian angel or any angel you wish to connect with—if you have doubt, a question, or a problem. They will point you in one way or another, and show you the right way to find a solution.

Unlike the classic tarot, the oracle deck of the angels creates a special bond with the querent. The angels manifest themselves to us and send messages, especially your guardian angel who is linked to you from birth. You will not only find answers to your questions but you will also create a strong bond with your heavenly protectors. It is up to you to follow their advice and let yourself be guided by their suggestions.

What are angels?

The 72 angels of Kabbalah, also referred to as the 72 names of God, have their origin in Jewish culture. Each angel is an expression of a divine quality—well-being, peace, and love— and of particular gifts and talents.

The angels are not beings with wings, as we traditionally imagine them. They are linked to very high vibrations of energy from God, subtle energies which are imperceptible to the naked eye but which still act on us. (This is reflected in the artworks on the cards, which depict the angels with their bright, powerful auras rather than as winged figures.) These 72 frequencies of energy surround the 360 degrees of the orbit that Earth makes around the Sun. This means that every five days, five degrees of the zodiacal circle is ruled by a specific angel. The angel that was ruling Earth on the day we were born is our guardian angel, and our character, potential, and life will be structured according to that angel's divine qualities. So by discovering the guardian angel that belongs to us, we are also able to understand the intent behind the physical structure of our life, and our higher qualities on a personal level.

The guardian angel in Kabbalah is also referred to as "the Angel of the Incarnation," and it tells us what we have come to manifest in life and reveals our purpose. Knowing our angel helps us understand how we work on an energetic level and what we need to change within us to transcend to a higher state of being.

When we invoke the names of the angels (see page 9), it allows us to let them enter our energy system in order to transform ourselves, to have greater balance and more inner peace, and it incarnates their qualities within us.

Who is your guardian angel?

Knowing your guardian angel means knowing yourself and your superior virtues. The artworks of the angels in this deck of cards reflect these virtues and how they are expressed in human beings.

The 72 guardian angels are grouped in the angelic calendar. Similar to the zodiac signs that change every month, the guardian angels change every five days. To find your guardian angel, you just need to know the month and day of your birth, then refer to the chart on pages 6–7.

Zodiac sign	Date	Guardian angel
Guardian angels of Aries	March 21–25	Vehuiah
	March 26–30	Jeliel
	March 31–April 4	Sitael
	April 5–9	Elemiah
	April 10–14	Mahasiah
	April 15–20	Lelahel
Guardian angels of Taurus	April 21–25	Achaiah
	April 26–30	Cahetel
	May 1–5	Haziel
	May 6–10	Aladiah
	May 11–15	Lauviah
	May 16–20	Hahaiah
Guardian angels of Gemini	May 21–25	Iezalel
	May 26–31	Mebahel
	June 1–5	Hariel
	June 6–10	Hekamiah
	June 11–15	Lauviah (II)
	June 16–21	Caliel
Guardian angels of Cancer	June 22–26	Leuviah
	June 27–July 1	Pahaliah
	July 2–6	Nelkhael
	July 7–11	Yeiayel
	July 12–16	Melahel
	July 17–22	Haheuiah
Guardian angels of Leo	July 23–27	Nith-Haiah
	July 28–August 1	Haaiah
	August 2–6	Yerathel
	August 7–12	Seheiah
	August 13–17	Reiyel
	August 18–22	Omael
Guardian angels of Virgo	August 23–28	Lecabel
	August 29–September 2	Vasariah
	September 3–7	Yehuiah
	September 8–12	Lehahiah
	September 13–17	Chavakhiah
	September 18–23	Menadel

Zodiac sign	Date	Guardian angel
Guardian angels of Libra	September 24–28	Aniel
	September 29–October 3	Haamiah
	October 4–8	Rehael
	October 9–13	Yeiazel
	October 14–18	Hahahel
	October 19–23	Mikael
Guardian angels of Scorpio	October 24–28	Veuliah
	October 29–November 2	Yelahiah
	November 3–7	Sehaliah
	November 8–12	Ariel
	November 13–17	Asaliah
	November 18–22	Mihael
Guardian angels of Sagittarius	November 23–27	Vehuel
	November 28–December 2	Daniel
	December 3–7	Hahasiah
	December 8–12	Imamiah
	December 13–16	Nanael
	December 17–21	Nithael
Guardian angels of Capricorn	December 22–26	Mebahiah
	December 27–31	Poyel
	January 1–5	Nemamiah
	January 6–10	Yeialel
	January 11–15	Harahel
	January 16–20	Mitzrael
Guardian angels of Aquarius	January 21–25	Umabel
	January 26–30	Iah-Hel
	January 31–February 4	Anauel
	February 5–9	Mehiel
	February 10–14	Damabiah
	February 15–19	Manakel
Guardian angels of Pisces	February 20–24	Eyael
	February 25–29	Habuhiah
	March 1–5	Rochel
	March 6–10	Jabamiah
	March 11–15	Haiaiel
	March 16–20	Mumiah

Angelic choirs

Every guardian angel belongs to an angelic choir, each of which has a particular job or purpose.

Angelic choir	Function
Seraphim	They purify all things
Cherubim	They are guardian angels of the light and stars
Thrones	They transmit the light that allows us to understand the trials of life
Dominations	They oversee the duties of the lower angels
Powers	They are warrior angels whose mission is to fight evil
Virtues	They can suspend the laws of nature to work miracles on Earth
Principalities	Their main mission is to bring harmony between the four elements—fire, earth, air, and water— and they are bearers of the gift of balance
Archangels	They manifest God's authority and directly transmit God's announcements to human beings
Angels	They manifest God's protection over all creatures; they are concerned with the evolution and protection of human beings from all the dangers that threaten them

Connecting with angels

The angels help us on a long journey of self-transformation, which will last a lifetime. When you achieve harmony with them, they will become your closest and most reliable friends. The more you invoke and thank your angels, the more you will receive and be surrounded by unimaginable love and joy.

Invoking your angel's name

The angels manifest only when their names are invoked. You can do this by whispering the name of the angel you wish to connect with, or we can invoke them just by thinking of their names with our heart. You may also listen to or sing sweet, gentle songs to invoke the angel.

The pronunciation of each angel's name is provided with its description on pages 16–158. For example, Vehuiah is pronounced "wah-heh-wah."

Connecting through meditation

You can connect to your angels through meditation. Here's how to prepare for meditation and get closer to your guardian angel or any of the angels within the deck.

1   Find a calm, quiet place where you feel protected and safe.
2   Focus on your breathing: inhale and exhale deeply, following the air as it enters your nostrils, passes through your windpipe, and fills your lungs. Focus on the flow of your breath.
3   Now focus on your soul: clear your mind and let yourself go. Bring to mind your chosen angel, repeating its name in your head. Open your heart and mind, and connect your spirit to your angel.
4   End the meditation by thanking the angel and saying goodbye to it.

Through this practice, you will raise your consciousness to a higher level of understanding and wisdom. You will discover communication with your angel in various ways, including through dreams, by noticing double and triple numbers anywhere they appear (for example, on your watch), or through any kind of synchronicity that we commonly call coincidence.

Using the angel cards

You can use your angel cards in various ways to communicate with your angels for help, guidance, and insight.

The one-card method

This simple method allows you to request help from the angels for something you desire.

Focus on your wish and ask a clear and precise question in your head, or out loud if you prefer, while holding the cards. Now shuffle the cards, concentrating on them very intensely and asking which angel can most help you at that moment. Then, keeping the cards face down, choose a card from the deck that you are instinctively drawn to. This card shows your angel of the day.

After choosing your card, enter a state of deep meditation, then invoke the angel, thinking of its name (see page 9). Call the angel with a heart full of love and a desire to feel its presence. Each angel has its own personality: some are sweet and kind, others strong and energetic.

Try to hear the angel's words of wisdom. Read the section dedicated to the selected angel on pages 16–158 to find out all its characteristics and what it can give you.

Finally, ask the angel for help in order to be able to fully receive the gift offered to you, then place the angel card in a place where you can look at it throughout the day.

The angelic gift: three-card spread

With this spread you can ask your angels to help you solve a problem.

Shuffle the cards with your question in mind to analyze your problem. When you feel ready, keeping the cards face down, choose three cards that you are instinctively drawn to. Arrange them in a row as shown below.

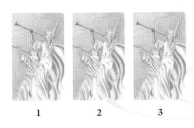

1   2   3

Turn over the cards, one at a time, and interpret them according to the guide below.

1   **The present:** The first angel will help you understand what influences are involved in the issue to be evaluated.

2   **The challenge:** The second angel helps you understand what is deep within your issue. It helps you identify the challenge—that is, the opportunity that presents itself to you—and perceive the deep feeling that characterizes the event in question.

3   **The gift:** The third angel brings you a gift to help you understand and respond positively to a new opportunity. Open your heart to the creative solutions and blessings the angel offers you.

The divine plan: eight-card spread

This powerful tool helps you channel your thoughts and feelings into angelic harmony.

Shuffle the deck while focusing on your problem. Keeping the cards face down, choose eight cards that you are instinctively drawn to. Arrange them face down as shown below.

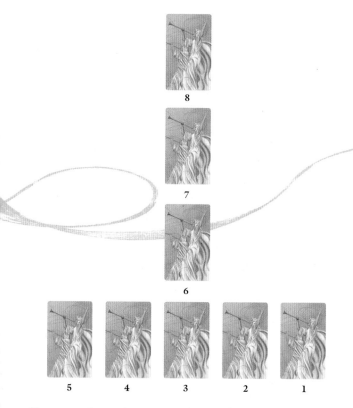

Turn over the cards, one at a time, and interpret them according to the guide opposite.

1   **The present:** Examine carefully what the angel has to tell you about your situation. How can the angel help you? What advice and wisdom is it giving you?

2   **The challenge:** What is your current challenge? What do you have to fight? Recognize the blessings that come in the form of challenges: they help you identify the illusions that prevent you from fully awakening. Listen to the advice that the angel gives you so that you will be able to understand and manage the challenge.

3   **The mind of the angel:** The blessing of this angel consists in shifting the consciousness of your limited self to the eternal one, from small everyday problems to the glorious expression of unconditional love. This angel helps you to recognize and overcome challenges.

4   **The liberation:** What are you afraid of releasing? What is holding you back? This angel represents a limitation, a judgment that you are ready to free yourself from.

5   **Your wisdom:** You already know and perceive much more than you realize. This angel is here to help you claim your wisdom and recognize your progress and talents.

6   **Your talents and skills:** Everything you have done and learned in life is in preparation for the fulfillment of the divine plan. This angel will help you integrate your spiritual desires with the material abilities that you have.

7   **The message:** This angel offers a message as a blessing to encourage you.

8   **The gift:** It is up to you to understand the meaning of the gift offered to you by the angel.

Examine how all the angels work together to help you. Pay attention to every thought and every sensation; you can also write in a notebook the inspiration and wise ideas you receive.

The kiss of the guardian angel: five-card spread

The following layout offers deep insight into your current situation, with the added wisdom of your guardian angel working with you.

Begin by identifying the card of your guardian angel (see pages 6–7) and read all its characteristics and meanings (see pages 16–158). Connect with your angel by invoking its name with intense desire (see page 9). When you have made contact, ask your angel to give you its wisdom. Ask the question you care about and return the card to the deck.

Shuffle the cards, focusing on how you are feeling now. Keeping the cards face down, choose five cards that you are instinctively drawn to. Arrange them face down as shown below.

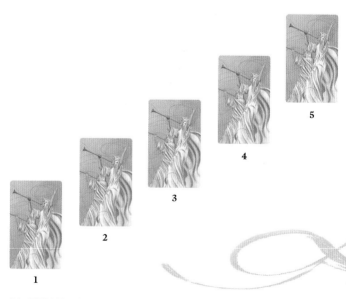

5

4

3

2

1

Turn over the cards, one at a time, and interpret them according to the guide below. Ask your guardian angel to reveal to you the way each angel works with it to help you. If your guardian angel appears as one of these cards, it suggests its meaning is of even greater importance to you.

1 **The present:** What's going on in your life? Examine your situation with a conscious attitude. Reflect on how this relates to your spiritual path. How can this angel help you?

2 **The next step:** What should you do next? This angel will help you with a gift. Meditate with the card, allowing yourself to enter a state of deep tranquility, in order to understand its meaning (see page 9).

3 **The liberation:** What old feelings and memories are constantly recurring in your life? This is a sign that it is time to get rid of them. Look at the qualities of the angel to understand which characteristics and behaviors you can use to free yourself from your situation.

4 **The gift:** This angel offers a message that will give you the strength to be free from all limitations.

5 **The kiss of your guardian angel:** This is the ultimate message of this reading and shows what this angel can give you. Read in detail all the qualities and abilities of the angel—these are the superior qualities, such as inspiration or courage, that you can have, if you want them.

1 Vehuiah

1 Vehuiah

The Voice of God

Guardian angel dates: March 21–25

Pronunciation: wah-heh-wah

Zodiac sign: Aries

Angelic choir: Seraphim

Associations and qualities
- Spiritual enlightenment
- Reasoning and introspection
- Calming anger
- Good health and healing
- Leadership
- Energy and strength
- Courage and audacity
- Success for all new creations
- Unprecedented and avant-garde work
- Removing confusion
- Self-worth and the value of others
- Concentration and focus

2 Jeliel

The Charitable God

Guardian angel dates: March 26–30

Pronunciation: yoh-LIE-yoh

Zodiac sign: Aries

Angelic choir: Seraphim

Associations and qualities
- Love and wisdom
- Charitable spirit
- Fruitfulness of people, animals, and plants
- Conjugal peace and fidelity
- Luck in business
- Protection from those with bad intentions
- Mediation and conciliation
- Loyalty
- Settlement of quarrels and conflicts
- Tranquility and a harmonious life
- Conviction and clarity

2 Jeliel

3
Sitael

3 Sitael

The God of Hope

Guardian angel dates: March 31–April 4

Pronunciation: sie-yoh-teh

Zodiac sign: Aries

Angelic choir: Seraphim

Assocations and qualities
- Protection against adversities and evil
- Physical strength and courage
- High science
- Planning, strategy, and common sense
- Honesty and faithfulness
- Responsibility and divine service
- Social and political notoriety
- Fruitfulness—conception of a child or a project
- Overcoming difficulties
- Awareness of mistakes to transform karma
- Nobility, magnanimity, generosity, and clemency
- Peacemaking and negotiations

4 Elemiah

The Hidden God

Guardian angel dates: April 5–9

Pronunciation: ah-lah-meh

Zodiac sign: Aries

Angelic choir: Seraphim

Associations and qualities
- Divine power
- Impartial authority
- Study and revelation of the life plan
- Protection from theft and accidents while traveling
- Inner peace
- Success and luck in the world of science
- Discovery of a new path
- Taking action and making decisions
- Career guidance
- Initiative, commitment, and enterprise
- Optimism at the end of a difficult period
- Identification of those who have betrayed you to make peace with them

4
Elemiah

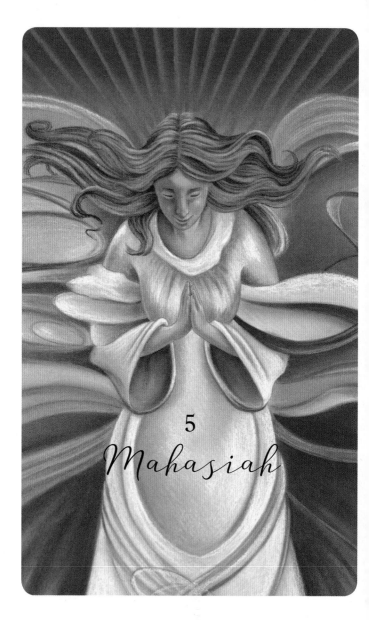

5

Mahasiah

5 *Mahasiah*

God the Savior

Guardian angel dates: April 10–14

Pronunciation: meh-heh-shee

Zodiac sign: Aries

Angelic choir: Seraphim

Associations and qualities

- Correction of errors
- Restoration of divine order
- Love of freedom
- Peace—enjoyment of simple and natural things
- Balance
- Diplomacy and wisdom
- Straightening that which grows distorted
- Learning (especially learning languages) and success in exams
- Decoding signs received in dreams and daily life
- Improvement of character
- Beautiful and happy existence

6 *Lelahel*

The Praiseworthy God

Guardian angel dates: April 15–20

Pronunciation: la-la-heh

Zodiac sign: Aries

Angelic choir: Seraphim

Associations and qualities

- The light of love—the divine light that heals everything
- Good health and fast healing from illness
- Spiritual enlightenment
- Natural beauty
- The mirror of the soul
- Fame and celebrity thanks to talent and personal achievements
- Success and luck in the world of science
- Lucidity and clarity of understanding
- Happiness and luck
- Self-expression
- Art and artists

6

Lelahel

7

Achaiah

7 Achaiah

The Forebearing and Patient God

Guardian angel dates: April 21–25

Pronunciation: ah-hah-ah

Zodiac sign: Taurus

Angelic choir: Seraphim

Associations and qualities

- Patience to overcome difficulties
- Truth and understanding
- Media—computers, television, radio, press, and publishing
- The secrets of nature and the meaning of life
- Ease in performing difficult work
- Intellectual activity, computer use, and programming
- Introspection—discovery of hidden aspects of yourself
- Desire to train and to learn
- Success in exams
- Solutions to difficult problems

8 Cahetel

The Adored God

Guardian angel dates: April 26–30

Pronunciation: kah-heh-tah

Zodiac sign: Taurus

Angelic choir: Seraphim

Associations and qualities
- Divine blessing and divine will
- Mysticism and introspection
- Patience
- Gratitude
- Birth and labour
- Wealth and abundance
- Cosmic laws and the four elements: fire, air, water, and earth
- Success and progress
- Agriculture, fertile lands, and abundant harvests
- Increased work capacity and an active life
- Nourishing the soul
- Overcoming evil spirits

8
Cahetel

9 Haziel

9 Haziel

The God of Mercy

Guardian angel dates: May 1–5

Pronunciation: eh-zy-oh

Zodiac sign: Taurus

Angelic choir: Cherubim

Associations and qualities
- Universal love and divine mercy
- Purity of childhood
- Goodness that absolves all evil
- Moral fiber and nobility
- Good faith, trust, generosity, and sincerity
- Transforming negativity
- Protection against envy
- Friendship and affection
- Wish fulfillment
- Promises and commitment
- Forgiveness and reconciliation
- Sympathy

10 *Aladiah*

The Favorable God

Guardian angel dates: May 6–10

Pronunciation: ah-lah-dah

Zodiac sign: Taurus

Angelic choir: Cherubim

Associations and qualities
- Divine grace that absolves and forgives all guilt
- Dissolution of karma
- Spiritual and material abundance
- Innocence
- Regeneration and thriving health
- Protection from evil forces
- Reintegration into society
- Great healing power
- Helping the needy
- Success at work
- Forgiveness

10
Aladiah

11

Lauviah

11 *Lauviah*

The Praised God

Guardian angel dates: May 11–15

Pronunciation: lah-hah-wah

Zodiac sign: Taurus

Angelic choir: Cherubim

Associations and qualities

- The light of God
- Passionate love of divine work
- Cosmic organization
- Resilience and victory
- Devotion and trust
- Great wisdom and diplomacy
- Protection of rulers and leaders
- Balance
- Fame, celebrity, and success
- Business that is useful and beneficial to humanity
- Selflessness, goodness, and kindness
- Enthusiasm and joy

12 *Hahaiah*

God the Refuge

Guardian angel dates: May 16–20

Pronunciation: eh-heh-hah

Zodiac sign: Taurus

Angelic choir: Cherubim

Associations and qualities
- Mediumship and interpretation of dreams
- Protection from the resentment of others
- Inner strength
- Peace, sleep, refuge, calm, and rest
- Meditation and love of solitude
- Cleanliness and tidiness
- Regaining and renewing energy
- Balance between intimate life and social life
- Calming aggression and destructive tendencies
- Personal-life examination
- Positive attitude
- Discretion

12 Hahaiah

13 Jezalel

13 *Iezalel*

The Glorified God

Guardian angel dates: May 21–25

Pronunciation: io-zah-lah

Zodiac sign: Gemini

Angelic choir: Cherubim

Associations and qualities
- Faithful servant
- Faithfulness to divine principles
- Friendship, loyalty, reunions, and meetings
- Happy memories
- Marital fidelity
- Reconciliation
- Learning
- Unity and union
- Balancing masculine and feminine aspects
- Order and harmony
- Carrying out projects
- Optimism

14 Mebahel

God the Protector and Savior

Guardian angel dates: May 26–31

Pronunciation: meh-beh-heh

Zodiac sign: Gemini

Angelic choir: Cherubim

Associations and qualities

- Inspiration that comes from higher worlds
- Commitment
- Humanitarian aid and altruism
- Truth, freedom, and justice
- Unconditional love
- Fairness, exactness, accuracy, precision, and right choices
- Restoration of natural order
- Adventure
- Renewal of hope
- Respect for the environment
- Mediation, conciliation, and arbitration
- Abundance and wealth
- Elevation of the senses

14
Mebahel

15 Hariel

15 *Hariel*

The Comforting God

Guardian angel dates: June 1–5

Pronunciation: heh-reh-oh

Zodiac sign: Gemini

Angelic choir: Cherubim

Associations and qualities
- Purification
- Purity of morals and innocence
- Spiritual feelings
- Supernatural forces
- Balance and happiness in family life
- Creativity and inventiveness at work
- Inspiration in science and art
- Divine laws and knowledge
- Lucidity and discernment
- Individuality and personality
- Freedom from whatever is paralyzing you
  and preventing you from acting
- Freedom from all forms of addiction

16 Hekamiah

God of the Universe

Guardian angel dates: June 6–10

Pronunciation: heh-KOH-meh

Zodiac sign: Gemini

Angelic choir: Cherubim

Associations and qualities
- Loyalty to divine principles
- Nobility
- Universal love
- Friendship
- Coordination, peacemaking, and liberation
- Commitment
- Frankness
- Accountability
- Leadership
- Political and social organizations
- Advice, intuition, and wisdom
- Protection from disputes

16 Hekamiah

17
Lauviah (II)

17 *Lauviah* (II)

The Admirable God

Guardian angel dates: June 11–15

Pronunciation: lah-HAH-wah

Zodiac sign: Gemini

Angelic choir: Thrones

Associations and qualities
- Mysteries of the universe and cosmic laws
- Rest and premonitory dreams
- Recovery from physical illness
- Relief from emotional and spiritual suffering
- Trustworthy friends
- Affection
- Revelations
- Intuitive understanding and telepathy
- Knowledge of the mechanisms of the psyche
- Joy and spiritual ascension
- Music, poetry, literature, and philosophy
- High science

18 Caliel

The God Who Fulfills

Guardian angel dates: June 16–21

Pronunciation: kah-lie-yoh

Zodiac sign: Gemini

Angelic choir: Thrones

Associations and qualities
- Absolute truth
- Elimination of all doubt
- Exoneration and regaining innocence
- Divine justice and karmic vision
- Interaction between good and evil
- Love of justice and perfect judgment
- Integrity and honesty
- Peace, tranquility, and inner well-being
- Ability to intuit intentions
- Protection from adversity
- Implementation of projects
- Eloquence

18 Caliel

19
Leuviah

19 *Leuviah*

The Swiftly Listening God

Guardian angel dates: June 22–26

Pronunciation: lah-wah-wah

Zodiac sign: Cancer

Angelic choir: Thrones

Associations and qualities
- Cosmic memory and memory of previous lives
- Expansive intelligence
- Amazing memory
- Communication
- Modesty
- Generosity
- Enduring adversity and mastering emotions
- Helping those in need
- Inner serenity
- Protection from accidents
- Recovery from illness
- Propensity for art

20 Pahaliah

God the Redeemer

Guardian angel dates: June 27–July 1

Pronunciation: peh-heh-lah

Zodiac sign: Cancer

Angelic choir: Thrones

Associations and qualities
- Liberation of the soul
- Transcendence of sexuality
- Purity in intimacy and divine sexual fusion
- Loyalty and fidelity
- Kundalini energy (life force)
- Sacrifices and redemption
- Instinctive behavior
- Courage and dynamism
- The higher self
- Harmonious spiritual life
- Propensity for science

20 *Pahaliah*

21 *Nelkhael*

21 Nelkhael

The Only God

Guardian angel dates: July 2–6

Pronunciation: neh-lah-fah

Zodiac sign: Cancer

Angelic choir: Thrones

Associations and qualities
- Cosmic organization
- Learning, study, and success in exams
- Omniscience
- Moving from concrete to abstract, from reality to idea
- Science, technology, and poetry
- Geometry, astronomy, astrology, and mathematics
- Scholars and philosophers
- Concentration
- Protection against slander, traps, and spells
- Exorcism through knowledge
- Teacher—pedagogue par excellence
- Protection from the forces of evil and envy

22 *Yeiayel*

The Right Hand of God

Guardian angel dates: July 7–11

Pronunciation: yoh-yoh-yoh

Zodiac sign: Cancer

Angelic choir: Thrones

Associations and qualities
- Fame and celebrity
- Patronage and philanthropy
- Political, artistic, and scientific activities
- Generosity and selflessness
- Respect for others
- Encouraging goodness
- Command, leadership, and diplomacy
- Luck and prosperity in business, trade, and travel
- Protection from unforeseen events and economic setbacks
- Surprising discoveries
- Resilience against illness

22 Yeiayel

23 Melahel

23 *Melahel*

God the Liberator

Guardian angel dates: July 12–16

Pronunciation: meh-lah-heh

Zodiac sign: Cancer

Angelic choir: Thrones

Associations and qualities

- Protection against weapons, fire, and attacks
- Healing
- Naturopathy, herbal medicine, and all natural sciences
- Travel
- Prosperity
- Happy marriage
- Healthy nutrition
- Appreciation and gratitude for divine abundance
- Faith and knowledge
- Adaptation and mastery of emotions
- Environmental protection and respect for nature
- Peace and relaxation

24 Hahewiah

The Good God

Guardian angel dates: July 17–22

Pronunciation: heh-heh-wah

Zodiac sign: Cancer

Angelic choir: Thrones

Associations and qualities
- Protection while traveling
- Honesty and incorruptibility
- Restoration of justice and stopping evil
- Police, army, advocacy, and judiciary
- Protection against thieves and murderers, demonic forces and spells, and dangerous or harmful animals
- Protection of exiles and immigrants
- Return to country of origin
- Sincerity and truth
- End of a difficult period
- Intuition
- Loyalty and lovable character
- Repairing karma

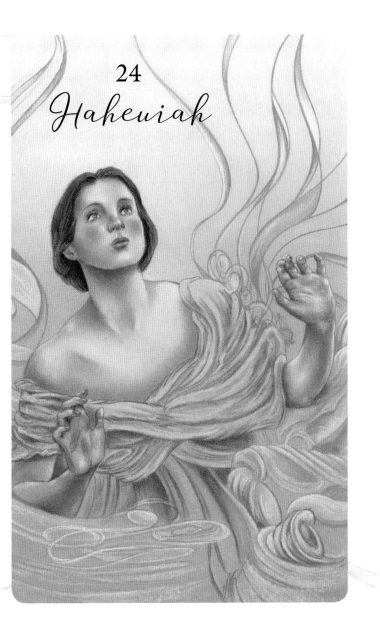

24
Haheuiah

25

Nith-Haiah

25 Nith-Haiah

The God of Wisdom

Guardian angel dates: July 23–27

Pronunciation: noo-tah-heh

Zodiac sign: Leo

Angelic choir: Thrones

Associations and qualities
- Esoteric disciplines
- Wisdom and love of study
- Protection from the forces of evil
- Good health
- Understanding of the notion of time
- Discovery of the hidden mysteries of creation
- Visions and revelations from dreams
- Meditation
- Peace, solitude, and silence
- Magic used only for good purposes
- Desire for the well-being of others
- Spiritual charisma

26 Haaiah

God Listening in Concealment

Guardian angel dates: July 28–August 1

Pronunciation: HEH-hah-hah

Zodiac sign: Leo

Angelic choir: Dominations

Associations and qualities
- Propensity for justice and the law
- Truth
- Great inner strength
- Discretion and counsel
- Power and abundance
- Secret information and knowledge
- Family and social circle
- Adaptation
- Propensity for science and politics
- Leadership, administration, decision making, diplomacy, and ambassadorship
- Behavior in ambiguous situations
- Positive, constructive atmosphere and team spirit

26 Haaiah

27 Yerathel

27 *Yerathel*

God the Protector

Guardian angel dates: August 2–6

Pronunciation: yoh-reh-tah

Zodiac sign: Leo

Angelic choir: Dominations

Associations and qualities

- Protection from enemies
- Eloquence
- Confidence
- Inexhaustible energy
- Propagation of God's light
- Optimism
- Teaching through speech and writing
- Sociability and being civilized
- Justice
- Science, literature, and the arts
- Dispelling confusion
- Success and progress

28 Seheiah

The God Who Heals

Guardian angel: August 7–12

Pronunciation: CHEE-hah-heh

Zodiac sign: Leo

Angelic choir: Dominations

Associations and qualities
- Excellent health
- Miraculous healing and rehabilitation
- Long and rewarding life
- Predisposition for medicine
- Protection from fire, accidents, and unpredictable events
- Friendship
- Foresight and premonition
- Lived experience
- Inspiration
- Prudence
- Calm

28
Seheiah

29 *Reiyel*

29 Reiyel
The Rescuer God

Guardian angel dates: August 13–17

Pronunciation: reh-yoh-yoh

Zodiac sign: Leo

Angelic choir: Dominations

Associations and qualities
- Protection from enemies, evil, and spells
- Comfort
- Health and quick recovery from illness
- Liberation
- Nature, wide open spaces, and high mountains
- Meditation and self-study
- Trust
- Global vision
- Search for truth
- Conception, realization, and production
- Divine work
- Bond with spiritual guides

30 Omael

The Patient God

Guardian angel dates: August 18–22

Pronunciation: ah-wah-meh

Zodiac sign: Leo

Angelic choir: Dominations

Associations and qualities

- Patience
- Protection from despair and sorrow
- The plant and animal kingdoms
- Nobility
- Materialization, development, and expansion
- Production, implementation, application, and planning
- Responsibility
- Healing and restoration of health
- Fruitfulness and birth
- Growth, bloom, and joy
- Cultivation and harvest
- Rediscovery of inner child

30 Omael

31 *Lecabel*

31 *Lecabel*

The Inspiring God

Guardian angel dates: August 23–28

Pronunciation: lah-hah-veh

Zodiac sign: Virgo

Angelic choir: Dominations

Associations and qualities
- The plant kingdom
- Intuition
- Success in professional work
- Overcoming difficulties
- Intelligence and lucidity
- Accuracy and precision
- Excellence and order at all levels
- Practical solutions
- Mastering emotions with reason
- Strategy, planning, management, engineering, and architecture
- Decisions and creations
- Exact mathematical sciences
- Bright and abundant ideas

32 Vasariah

The Right God

Guardian angel dates: August 29–September 2

Pronunciation: wah-shee-reh

Zodiac sign: Virgo

Angelic choir: Dominations

Associations and qualities
- Justice
- Nobility and righteousness
- Judicary and law
- Protection from aggression and backbiting
- Overcoming difficulties
- Clemency and forgiveness
- Great wisdom
- Planning, organization, problem solving, and strategy
- Goodness, benevolence, kindness, and magnanimity
- Modesty
- Oratory talent
- Listening, compassion, and empathy

32 Vasariah

33

Yehuiah

33 Yehuiah
The All-Knowing God

Guardian angel dates: September 3–7

Pronunciation: yoh-HEH-wah

Zodiac sign: Virgo

Angelic choir: Powers

Associations and qualities
- Protection against hostility, envy, and conspiracies
- Success at work
- Science and scientific discoveries
- Just and constructive high-level leadership
- Team spirit, alliance, and collaboration
- Planning and responsibility
- Honesty, trust, and loyalty
- Easing tension
- Awareness of one's place in the cosmic order
- Exposing traitors
- Altruism, philanthropy, and duty
- Commitment and contracts

34 Lehahiah

The Clement God

Guardian angel dates: September 8–12

Pronunciation: lah-heh-HEH

Zodiac sign: Virgo

Angelic choir: Powers

Associations and qualities
- Calming anger
- Obedience
- Trust and favor of superiors
- Discipline and sense of order
- Loyalty, dedication, devotion, selfless actions, and faithfulness
- Divine laws and justice
- Dedication to service
- Government, ministry, presidentship, and directorship
- Intelligence
- Peace and harmony, the ability to be at ease in ambiguity
- Incorruptibility and integrity
- Acceptance of destiny

34
Lehahiah

35 *Chavakhiah*

35 Chavakhiah

The God of Joy

Guardian angel dates: September 13–17

Pronunciation: kah-wah-keh

Zodiac sign: Virgo

Angelic choir: Powers

Associations and qualities
- Easygoing character
- Overcoming difficulties
- Protection from discord
- Forgiveness and reconciliation
- Harmonious family relationships
- Trust, help, and support from family
- Ancestral wisdom
- Reconnection
- Human and social sciences
- Peace and mediation
- Loyalty
- Inheritance, distribution of assets, and gifts

36 Menadel

The Honorable God

Guardian angel dates: September 18–23

Pronunciation: meh-NOOR-dah

Zodiac sign: Virgo

Angelic choir: Powers

Associations and qualities

- Medicine and healing
- Advice
- Luck in changes of residence
- Helpfulness
- Vocation, career, and finding a job
- Cooperation, availability, and altruism
- Truth and freedom found in work
- Inner work
- Willpower
- Discovering potential
- Dedication and devotion

36 Menadel

37 Aniel

37 Aniel

God, Lord of All Virtues

Guardian angel dates: September 24–28

Pronunciation: ah-noor-yoh

Zodiac sign: Libra

Angelic choir: Powers

Assocations and qualities
- The secrets of nature and concepts of the universe
- Cycles of life and evolution
- Science
- Overcoming adversities
- Breaking old patterns
- History—causes and consequences
- Karma and reaping what one sows
- Novelty, change of mentality, and new ideas
- Independence and spiritual autonomy
- Freedom from emotional dependence and all other forms of addiction
- Mastery of intense intellectual and emotional impulses
- Protection against negative forces and emotions

38 Haamiah

God, Hope of All Which Ends the Earth

Guardian angel dates: September 29–October 3

Pronunciation: heh-heh-meh

Zodiac sign: Libra

Angelic choir: Powers

Associations and qualities
- Strategy and planning
- Taking care of others
- Highest human achievements
- Behavioral science
- Beauty, harmony, and peace
- Good education, courtesy, and conviviality
- Transcendence
- Dissolution of inner and outer violence
- Charisma, persuasion, and compliments
- Extraordinary love story
- Divine sexuality
- Mysticism and spiritual quest

38 Haamiah

39

Rehael

39 *Rehael*

The Forgiving God

Guardian angel dates: October 4–8

Pronunciation: reh-heh-hah

Zodiac sign: Libra

Angelic choir: Powers

Associations and qualities

- Healing mental illness, depression, and distress
- Protection from danger
- Friendship
- Loyalty in love
- Great sensitivity
- Humility
- Listening to others
- Trust of superiors
- Fatherly love
- Obedience and respect
- Regeneration

40 *Yeiazel*

The God Who Delights Every Living Thing

Guardian angel dates: October 9–13

Pronunciation: yoh-YOH-zah

Zodiac sign: Libra

Angelic choir: Powers

Associations and characteristics

- Joy
- Consolation and comfort
- Selflessness
- Protection against enemies
- Appreciation
- Restoration and revitalization of the body
- Prevention of emotional overflow
- Freedom from emotional conditioning and addiction of any kind
- End of a difficult time
- Peace and harmony
- Start of a new creation
- Writing, publishing, printing, bookselling, painting, and the arts

40
Yeiazel

41 *Hahahel*

41 *Hahahel*

The God of the Trinity

Guardian angel dates: October 14–18

Pronunciation: heh-heh-heh

Zodiac sign: Libra

Angelic choir: Virtues

Associations and qualities
- Dedicated and faithful servant
- Vocation based on spirituality
- Spiritual guide, shepherd of souls, and missionary
- Faith and spiritual wealth
- Protection against enemies of spirituality
- Sacrifice
- Leadership and wisdom
- Courage
- The meaning and purpose of life
- Knowledge and vision
- Meditation while in action
- Luck in travel and friendships

42 Mikael

The God of Virtue

Guardian angel dates: October 19–23

Pronunciation: meh-yoor-hah

Zodiac sign: Libra

Angelic choir: Virtues

Associations and qualities
- Diplomacy and success in politics
- Heaven on Earth
- Social and spiritual organization
- Wise and provident planning
- Knowledge of good and evil
- Clarity and global vision
- Longevity
- Discovery of secrets and mysteries
- Natural authority, obedience, and fidelity
- Presidentship, ministry, ambassadorship, consulship, management, and teaching
- Travel safety and security
- Protection from accidents

42
Mikael

43 Veuliah

43 *Veuliah*

The Ruler God

Guardian angel dates: October 24–28

Pronunciation: wah-wah-lah

Zodiac sign: Scorpio

Angelic choir: Virtues

Associations and qualities
- Protection from enemies
- Freedom from depression and loneliness
- Luck in career and business initiatives
- Prosperity, wealth, and abundance
- Joy
- Responsible, fair, and unselfish use of wealth
- Trade, business, finance, administration, and management
- Fruitfulness
- Natural authority
- Peace and fullness
- Vision, strategy, foresight, and planning
- Philanthropy

44 Yelahiah

God the Eternal

Guardian angel dates: October 29–November 2

Pronunciation: yoh-LAH-heh

Zodiac sign: Scorpio

Angelic choir: Virtues

Associations and qualities
- Universal protector and spiritual guide
- Divine justice
- Military talent
- Fight against adversity
- Resolution of conflict, victory, and establishment of peace
- Protection against injustice
- Resolution of karmic debts
- Self-assertion, courage, and audacity
- Openness and loyalty
- Success in enterprises
- Wisdom
- Leading and helping others

44
Yelahiah

45 *Sehaliah*

45 Sehaliah

The God Who Motivates

Guardian angel dates: November 3–7

Pronunciation: sah-HAH-lah

Zodiac sign: Scorpio

Angelic choir: Virtues

Associations and qualities
- Healing and recovery from illness
- Kindness
- Motivation and pure intentions
- Will, concentration, and focus
- Ardor, enthusiasm, and hope
- Impulse and awakening
- New beginning
- Enhancing consciousness
- Balance of life force
- Master of the four elements: fire, air, water, and earth
- Protection from treachery

46 *Ariel*

The Revealing God

Guardian angel dates: November 8–12

Pronunciation: ah-reh-yoh

Zodiac sign: Scorpio

Angelic choir: Virtues

Associations and qualities

- The secrets of nature
- Science, medicine, and research
- Clear mind
- Perception and intuition
- Protection from accidents
- Mediumship, clairvoyance, and clairaudience
- Hidden treasure
- Meditation, dreams, and signs
- Gratitude
- Subtlety and discretion
- Invention and new ideas
- Philosophical secrets

46 *Ariel*

47 Asaliah

47 *Asaliah*

The God of Truth

Guardian angel dates: November 13–17

Pronunciation: ah-shee-lah

Zodiac sign: Scorpio

Angelic choir: Virtues

Associations and qualities
- Cosmic processes, esoteric disciplines, and paranormal faculties
- Understanding, contemplation, and deep thought
- Divine and mystical experience
- Global perspective
- Psychology
- Instruction, teaching, strategy, and planning
- Access to parallel worlds
- Meditation, visualization, and mantras
- Mental power, concentration, and focus
- Spiritual consciousness and a sense of the sacred
- High morality, integrity, and authentic and true values
- Respect and fidelity within couples

48 Mihael

God the Father and the Charitable

Guardian angel dates: November 18–22

Pronunciation: meh-yoh-heh

Zodiac sign: Scorpio

Angelic choir: Virtues

Associations and qualities
- Love, peace, and kindness
- Trusted friendships
- Family and children
- Fertility and growth
- Marital harmony and fidelity
- Fusion of masculine and feminine polarities
- Great soul
- Divine sexuality
- Associations and collaborations
- Clairvoyance and perception
- Providential protection
- Receptivity and listening

48 Mihael

49 Vehuel

49 *Vehuel*

The Great and Exalted God

Guardian angel dates: November 23–27

Pronunciation: wah-heh-wah

Zodiac sign: Sagittarius

Angelic choir: Principalities

Associations and qualities
- Dedication, selflessness, and generosity
- Protection from theft and accidents
- Divine greatness and wisdom
- Meditation, visualization, and mantras
- Access to parallel worlds
- Illumination and inspiration
- Detachment from material things
- Sensitivity and diplomacy
- Freedom from instinctive desires
- Fraternity and humanitarian aid
- Aspiration
- Writing

50 *Daniel*

God the Merciful Judge

Guardian angel dates: November 28–December 2

Pronunciation: dah-noor-yoh

Zodiac sign: Sagittarius

Angelic choir: Principalities

Associations and qualities
- Reasoning
- Beauty and art
- Consolation and helping others
- Protection from attackers
- Eloquence and expressiveness
- Communication
- Leadership and inspiring others
- Thoughtfulness and kindness
- Goodness and harmony
- Clarity and decisions
- Materialization of thoughts through actions
- Speech, singing, music, and the arts

50 *Daniel*

51 *Hahasiah*

51 Hahasiah

God the Impenetrable Secret

Guardian angel dates: December 3–7

Pronunciation: heh-HEH-shee

Zodiac sign: Sagittarius

Angelic choir: Principalities

Associations and qualities

- Wisdom
- Noble character
- Scientific research
- Protection from liars
- Health professions—medicine, nursing, neurobiology, and neurotechnology
- Global and multidimensional understanding
- True healing
- Infinite goodness
- Unconditional help
- The dynamics of the universe
- Esoteric knowledge—Kabbalah, alchemy, and metaphysics
- High soul

52 Imamiah

The High God

Guardian angel dates: December 8–12

Pronunciation: AH-meh-meh

Zodiac sign: Sagittarius

Angelic choir: Principalities

Associations and qualities
- Freedom and independence
- Success in business and society
- Memory
- Recognition of own mistakes
- Atonement, correction, and karma
- Courage, ardor, abundant vigor, and emotional strength
- Caring for, supporting, and comforting others
- Charisma and leadership
- Social and harmonious life
- Making peace with enemies
- Faithfulness, humility, and simplicity
- Patience

52 *Imamiah*

53 Nanael

53 Nanael

The God of Knowledge

Guardian angel dates: December 13–16

Pronunciation: NOOR-NOOR-ah

Zodiac sign: Sagittarius

Angelic choir: Principalities

Associations and qualities
- Occult sciences and esoteric knowledge
- Meditation
- Law and magistracy
- Truth
- Spiritual communication
- Abstract sciences and philosophy
- Spiritual life and teachings
- Mysticism
- Solitude
- Communication with the divine

54 Nithael

God the King of Heaven

Guardian angel dates: December 17–21

Pronunciation: noor-yoor-tah

Zodiac sign: Sagittarius

Angelic choir: Principalities

Associations and qualities
- Long and peaceful life
- Protection from danger
- Divine help in times of difficulty
- Mystical and noble soul
- Eternal youth
- Beauty, grace, and refinement
- Synchronicity and stability
- Hospitality and a warm welcome
- Artistic and aesthetic talents
- Celebrity and prestige
- Healing
- Inheritance and legitimate succession

54 *Nithael*

55
Mebahiah

55 Mebahiah

The Eternal God

Guardian angel dates: December 22–26

Pronunciation: meh-beh-heh

Zodiac sign: Capricorn

Angelic choir: Principalities

Associations and qualities

- Childhood
- Inner serenity
- Teaching
- Intellectual lucidity
- Generosity, goodness, and benevolence
- Adaptation and regulation of desires
- Duty and responsibility
- Opening the heart
- Consolation
- Deep and mystical spiritual experience and ideas
- Morality and exemplary behavior
- Commitment

56 Poyel

God Who Sustains Everything

Guardian angel dates: December 27–31

Pronunciation: FEH-why-oh

Zodiac sign: Capricorn

Angelic choir: Principalities

Associations and qualities

- Luck and success
- Support
- Modesty and simplicity
- Altruism
- The gifts of Providence
- Ideas and positive atmospheres
- Talent, fame, and celebrity lived with humility
- Healing, health, and well-being
- Eloquence and clear expression
- Peace and tranquility
- Hope and optimism
- Humor

56
Poyel

57 Nemamiah

57 Nemamiah

The Praiseworthy God

Guardian angel dates: January 1–5

Pronunciation: noor-meh-meh

Zodiac sign: Capricorn

Angelic choir: Archangels

Associations and qualities
- Taking control
- Advice
- Military life
- Justice
- Discernment and observation
- Anticipation and farsightedness
- Strategy, decisions, and action
- Devotion to great causes
- Greatness of mind
- Nobility of spirit
- Freedom
- Life plan

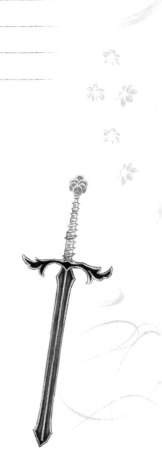

58 *Yeialel*

The Right Hand of God

Guardian angel dates: January 6–10

Pronunciation: YOOR-YOOR-lah

Zodiac sign: Capricorn

Angelic choir: Archangels

Associations and qualities
- Divine laws and structures
- Healing from illness, especially psychosomatic
- Protection from scammers and liars
- Art and beauty
- Patience, mental strength, concentration, and high-level intelligence
- Logic, precision, and rigorous discernment
- Awareness and clairvoyance
- Neurotechnology
- Computers and programming
- Frankness and audacity
- Justice and order
- Kindness and unconditional loyalty

58
Yeialel

59 Harahel

59 Harahel

The Omniscient God

Guardian angel dates: January 11–15

Pronunciation: heh-reh-HEH

Zodiac sign: Capricorn

Angelic choir: Archangels

Associations and qualities
- Mathematics and administration
- Calmness
- Wisdom and beauty
- Protection from fire and explosions
- Recovery from illness
- Knowledge and intellectual wealth
- Intellectual creativity and practical intelligence
- Goodness, honesty, and truth
- Education and learning
- Fruitfulness and productivity
- Obedience and respect for elders
- Writing, journalism, publishing, and printing

60 Mitzrael

The Rescuer God

Guardian angel dates: January 16–20

Pronunciation: meh-SAH-reh

Zodiac sign: Capricorn

Angelic choir: Archangels

Associations and qualities
- Studies and teaching
- Helpfulness and selflessness
- Healing
- Advice, comfort, and rescue
- Obedience and authority
- Correction and repair
- Psychology and psychiatry
- Neurobiology, neurotechnology, and technology in general
- Recovery from mental illness
- Intellectual work
- Reunification of the physical, emotional, mental, and spiritual planes
- Simplicity

60 Mitzrael

61 Umabel

61 *Umabel*

The Immense God

Guardian angel dates: January 21–25

Pronunciation: wah-meh-veh

Zodiac sign: Aquarius

Angelic choir: Archangels

Associations and qualities

- Friendship
- Learning and intelligence
- Technology and neurotechnology
- Recognition of subconscious motivations
- Physics, astronomy, and astrology
- In-depth understanding
- The mineral, plant, and animal kingdoms
- Consciousness
- Instruction and teaching
- Discovering the unknown

62 Jah-Hel

The Supreme God

Guardian angel dates: January 26–30

Pronunciation: YOH-heh-heh

Zodiac sign: Aquarius

Angelic choir: Archangels

Associations and qualities
- Responsibility, wisdom, and truth
- Modesty, sincerity, and loyalty
- Introspection and deep meditation
- Physical and mental well-being
- Illumination and newfound knowledge
- Philosophy and mysticism
- Solitude and tranquility
- Divine sexuality and pure pleasure
- Payment of karmic debts
- Clairvoyance and clairaudience
- Positive, harmonious atmosphere
- Beauty, poetry, and culinary art

62 Iah-Hel

63
Anauel

63 *Anauel*

The Gentle God

Guardian angel dates: January 31–February 4

Pronunciation: ah-noor-ah

Zodiac sign: Aquarius

Angelic choir: Archangels

Associations and qualities

- Protection against unexpected events and accidents
- Health
- Courage
- Responsibility, leadership, organization, and altruism
- Mysticism
- Success in art
- Relationships and communication
- Practical intelligence, logic, and global vision
- Money and exchanges
- New concepts, ideas, and technologies
- Administration, coordination, and planning
- Merchandise, banking, business, and industry

64 Mehiel

The Vivifying God

Guardian angel dates: February 5–9

Pronunciation: MEH-heh-yoh

Zodiac sign: Aquarius

Angelic choir: Archangels

Associations and qualities
- Self-expression through writing
- Success in business and through communication
- Protection against the forces of evil
- Inspiration and imagination
- Intense, fruitful, and productive life
- Intelligence, receptivity, and deep understanding
- Practical and innovative solutions
- Technological development, computer use, and programming
- Writing, publishing, printing, broadcasting houses, and libraries
- Reflection on personal experience

64 Mehiel

65
Damabiah

65 Damabiah

God the Source of Wisdom

Guardian angel dates: February 10–14

Pronunciation: dah-meh-beh

Zodiac sign: Aquarius

Angelic choir: Angels

Associations and qualities
- Wisdom and diplomacy
- Protection against bankruptcy
- Luck when traveling
- Maritime trade and fishing
- Activities related to water
- Purity, sweetness, and goodness
- Altruism and generosity
- Dedication and unconditional love
- Success in businesses useful to the community
- Emotions and feelings
- Resolution of compromised situations

66 Manakel

The Strength of God

Guardian angel dates: February 15–19

Pronunciation: meh-noor-keh

Zodiac sign: Aquarius

Angelic choir: Angels

Associations and qualities
- Calming and healing
- Strength
- Lasting friendship
- Finding work quickly
- Stability and trust
- Beautiful and harmonious life
- High morality
- Amiability, kindness, and benevolence
- Potential hidden in the depths
- Neurotechnology
- Dreams
- Reunification of body and spirit

66 Manakel

67

Eyael

67 *Eyael*

The God of Delights

Guardian angel dates: February 20–24

Pronunciation: ah-yoh-ah

Zodiac sign: Pisces

Angelic choir: Angels

Associations and qualities
- Protection from misfortune and unexpected events
- Wisdom and enlightenment
- Mysticism
- Transubstantiation, transfiguration, transformation, mutation, and metamorphosis
- Abstract truth transformed into concrete truth
- History, origin, and genesis
- Archeology
- Observation and perception
- Chemistry, physics, biology, biotechnology, and neurotechnology
- Culinary art, painting, and music
- Joy
- Solitude

68 Habuhiah

God the Liberator

Guardian angel dates: February 25–29

Pronunciation: heh-veh-wah

Zodiac sign: Pisces

Angelic choir: Angels

Associations and qualities

- Inner wealth
- Sociability
- Kindness and generosity
- Wisdom
- Abundance of material and spiritual crops
- Healing
- Medicine and therapy, including energetic, metaphysical, and spiritual healing
- Balance and regulation of desire
- Harmonization
- Nature, country life, and open spaces
- Agriculture, cultivation, and crops
- Fertile nature and creative power

68 Habuhiah

69 Rochel

69 *Rochel*

The All-Seeing God

Guardian angel dates: March 1–5

Pronunciation: reh-HAH-heh

Zodiac sign: Pisces

Angelic choir: Angels

Associations and qualities
- Physical strength
- Protection from theft and loss of assets
- Love and social relationships
- Historical studies
- Justice and laws
- Restitution and compensation
- Succession and inheritance
- Intuition
- History and practical and theoretical sciences
- Giving and receiving
- Administration and accounting
- Karma

70 Jabamiah

God the Creator

Guardian angel dates: March 6–10

Pronunciation: yoh-veh-meh

Zodiac sign: Pisces

Angelic choir: Angels

Associations and qualities
- Inner wealth
- Regeneration
- Quick recovery from illness
- Alchemy
- Love
- Healing
- Restoration of harmony
- Transmutation and transformation
- Bright ideas
- Accompaniment of the dying
- Parallel worlds
- Spiritual guidance and healing

70 Jabamiah

71

Haiaiel

71 Haiaiel

God of the Universe

Guardian angel dates: March 11–15

Pronunciation: heh-yoh-yoh

Zodiac sign: Pisces

Angelic choir: Angels

Associations and qualities
- Lucidity and discernment
- Protection at work
- Decisions
- Victory and peace
- Courage and strength of mind
- Receptive intelligence and strategy
- Freedom from oppressors
- Staying on or rediscovering the right path
- New ideas and concepts
- Receptivity to divine inspiration
- Great energy
- Leadership

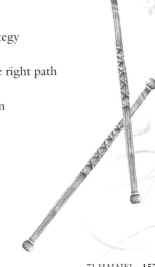

72 Mumiah

God the End of the Universe

Guardian angel dates: March 16–20

Pronunciation: meh-wah-meh

Zodiac sign: Pisces

Angelic choir: Angels

Associations and qualities

- Conclusions and completion of goals
- Serenity
- Enjoying small things
- The secrets of nature
- Lunar energies
- Rebirth and new beginnings
- Receptivity, mediumship, and mystical experiences
- Reincarnation
- Complete realization and materialization
- Medicine and health
- Accompaniment of the dying
- Consciousness

72 Mumiah

Resources

An audio guide to the names of the angels:
https://youtu.be/HAH9wrudFn4

Find Delia Ciccarelli on Instagram @deliaimagination.

Acknowledgments

I would like to thank and dedicate these angels to my family. I would also like to thank my little pigeon Sun, who keeps me company every day.